SPORTS GREAT ROGER CLEMENS

—*Sports Great Books*—

SPORTS GREAT ROGER CLEMENS

John Devaney

—Sports Great Books—

ENSLOW PUBLISHERS, INC.

Bloy St. & Ramsey Ave.   P.O. Box 38
Box 777   Aldershot
Hillside, N.J. 07205   Hants GU12 6BP
U.S.A.   U.K.

Library of Congress Cataloging-in-Publication Data

Devaney, John.
   Sports great Roger Clemens /by John Devaney.
      p. cm. — (Sports great books)
   Includes index.
   Summary: Follows the life of Boston Red Sox pitcher Roger
Clemens and his notable pitching accomplishments in his
chosen sport.
   ISBN 0-89490-284-9
   1. Clemens, Roger—Juvenile literature. 2. Baseball players—
United States—Biography—Juvenile literature. 3. Pitching
(Baseball)—Juvenile literature. 4. Boston Red Sox (Baseball
team)—Juvenile literature. [1. Clemens, Roger. 2. Baseball
players.]
   1. Title.   II. Series
GV865.C44D48   1990
796.357'092—dc20
[B]
[92]   89-7874
                            CIP
                            AC

Printed in the United States of America

10 9 8 7 6 5 4 3 2 1

Illustration Credits:
AP/Wide World Photos, pp. 9, 27, 31, 33, 35, 40, 41, 42, 48, 49, 51, 53, 56, 58, 60;
Larry Pierce, p. 23; Travis Spradling, p. 26; Photos by Roy Waldrep, pp. 15, 18,
21.

Cover Photo: AP/Wide World Photos

Contents

Chapter 1

The big-league scout stood in the living room. He held a piece of paper in his hand. "If you don't sign this contract," he said, "you will never get another chance to pitch in the big leagues."

Roger Clemens stared, his mouth dry. His mother told the scout that the offer of a thousand dollars was not enough. Anyway, she wanted Roger to go to college.

Seventeen-year-old Roger glanced at the paper. The scout saw the dreamy look on Roger's face. It was the same dreamy look he had seen on the faces of hundreds of teenage boys. It was the look of a boy who imagined himself in a big-league uniform.

"Last chance, son," the scout said.

Roger shook his head. He was saying no. The scout turned and walked out the door. The husky, six-foot Roger watched from a window as the scout walked down the street.

Roger said a quick goodbye to his mother. He jogged alone through the dark streets of Katy, Texas, a suburb of Houston. Roger stopped at a deserted baseball field. He stretched out on the pitcher's mound. He stared upward at the stars.

No one wanted him now. He was too old for Little League. He'd graduate next week from high school. His baseball coach had told him he didn't throw fast enough to pitch for a college team. And his dream of playing for a big-league team had just walked out the door.

Was that dream gone forever? No! He'd show 'em.

Roger stood up. He walked off the pitcher's mound into the darkness. He'd show that scout—and anyone else—that he could do what people said he couldn't do. He'd show 'em!

For two days after the scout left, Roger huddled in his locked bedroom. His face glum, he brooded about the scout's words, "Last chance, son." How could he show that the scout was wrong when he said that the thousand-dollar offer was Roger's "last chance?"

"You can't stay locked in that room forever, Roger."

Roger heard his mother's voice coming from the hallway. Roger walked to the door and opened it. His mother and older brother, Randy, stood in the hallway. Worry lined their faces.

Randy and his mother were the most important people in Roger's life. Roger was born on August 4, 1962, in Dayton, Ohio. His father, Bill Clemens, a truck driver, and his mother were divorced when Roger was three months old. Later, when Roger was five, his mother, Bess, married Woody Booher, a factory worker.

The family moved to Vandalia, Ohio, not far from Dayton. There were five children—Rick, Randy, Brenda, Janet, and Roger. They soon had a baby sister, Bonnie. A barn held four horses and a pony. Each child could ride his or her own horse. "Woody," Roger often said, "gave us everything we could have asked for."

Little did young Roger Clemens know that he would someday become this fearsome sight to a batter.

At six Roger liked to shoot at tin cans with a BB gun. At seven, bigger than most boys, he jumped astride Woody's motorcycle. He gripped his stepfather's waist, whooping and hollering. Woody drove the motorbike up and down dirt trails.

Roger often saw Randy's name in headlines on Vandalia sports pages. Randy scored twenty and thirty points in high school basketball games. "I want to play sports like Randy," Roger told his mother.

"You're only eight," she said. "You can't play Little League baseball until you're nine."

Randy told a Little League coach, "My kid brother is husky. He can throw a ball as fast as any ten-year-old."

The coach put Roger on his team. The stocky eight-year-old boy looked ten or eleven.

In Little League, Roger pitched against tall, muscled twelve-year-olds. "Get the ball over the plate, kid," the twelve-year-olds snarled.

Roger gulped. He aimed the ball so it streaked over the plate. The batters hit those straight pitches for doubles, triples, and homers.

Roger began to throw faster. His pitches still went straight over the plate. But they went so fast that they whizzed by the batters.

"The kid is pretty fast," one coach told Randy. "But lots of big kids are fast. What's good about Roger is, he hardly ever walks anyone."

One day, when Roger was nine, his mother came to a game. She watched Roger blaze nine straight strikes past three batters. Her eyes widened as she heard each pitch hit the catcher's mitt as loud as a gun's roar. That night she told Randy, "I think we have something special in the family."

Each night, after his homework, Roger stood in front of a tall mirror. He wound up and went through the motion of pitching. He watched the mirror to see that each part of his motion was as smooth as the motion of the big-league pitchers on TV. He read books on how to pitch.

He wanted to be a pitcher. He told Randy, "I want to be the guy whose name is on the line for the win or loss. A lot of eyes are on you all the time when you pitch. You've got to be good or your team loses. Guys say, 'Win the game for us, Roger.' I like that pressure."

Roger loved the family dinners. He and his brothers and sisters laughed as Woody told funny stories. One night Woody said he felt ill. He left the table and went to his bedroom.

An hour later Roger saw red lights swirling outside his window. He heard an ambulance's siren screaming.

"What's going on?" he asked his older sisters. An hour later he got the answer. A heart attack had killed Woody.

Randy gathered his brothers and sisters around him. "We've got to stick together as a family," Randy told them. "And we've get to help Mom."

Roger told himself that as soon as he was old enough, he'd get the best job he could to take care of his mother.

Bess worked as a bookkeeper at a local store. Randy won a scholarship and went to a college in Mississippi. He starred as a basketball high scorer. Then he and another brother, Rick, got high-paying jobs in Houston, Texas. They phoned their mother in Vandalia and told her, "Come to Texas."

Now almost thirteen years old, Roger towered over the other kids in his class. He stood almost six feet tall and weighed a beefy 165 pounds. In the fall he looked like a boulder on the defensive line of his high school football team. In the spring he pitched against sixteen-year-old hitters. In a seven-inning game he struck out nineteen of twenty-one batters.

"You've got to pitch against better hitters, Roger," Randy

said on the phone. "Here in Houston they play baseball in the spring, summer, fall, and winter. You can't do that in Ohio. I see high school pitchers throw 80 miles an hour. I see batters hit 80-mile-an-hour pitches for home runs."

Roger had read that Nolan Ryan, a fast-ball pitcher for the California Angels could throw 100.8 miles an hour—faster than anyone. Roger dreamed of one day throwing 100-mile-an-hour fireballs.

"Throw only fast balls," Randy told Roger. "Don't fool around with curves and other breaking pitches. They'll hurt your arm."

Years later Roger told Little Leaguers, "Throwing curves when you are only fourteen is dangerous. Those pitches will only wear out your arm. Concentrate on throwing fast balls for strikes."

Roger's mother worried about taking Roger and his older sisters out of high school in Vandalia and moving to Houston. She asked herself: Would the girls miss their friends? But she knew Roger wanted to join Randy in Houston.

One day—it was in the spring of 1976—she decided what to do. When Roger came home from school, she told Roger that she and the girls were staying in Vandalia for a while. But Roger would leave tomorrow for Houston—his future home—and the soon-to-be home of his idol Nolan Ryan.

In Houston Roger lived with Randy and Randy's wife. A schoolteacher, she helped Roger to study. After graduating from junior high school back in Vandalia, Roger now attended Dulles High in Houston as a sophomore. He pitched and played first base for Dulles. As a pitcher, he won twelve games and lost only one.

"My fast ball is getting close to 75 miles an hour," Roger told Randy.

"Dulles doesn't play real good teams," Randy said.

"I thought I was a hot-shot pitcher," Roger said later. His big brother's words took a lot of air out of him. You couldn't get a swelled head with Randy around.

In the fall of 1978, the sixteen-year-old Roger—now 220 pounds and six feet two—enrolled at Spring Woods High School. That fall Roger knifed through blockers to bowl over runners for the Spring Woods football team.

In the spring of 1979, though, the Spring Woods baseball coach, broad-shouldered Charley Miorana frowned when he saw Roger. "You're so fat," he told Roger, "you'll have trouble bending over to pick up ground balls."

The coach sent Roger to a fitness trainer. Roger jumped and twisted for hours. He kept a daily diary: how many miles he ran, what food he ate.

"Keep that diary," the trainer told him. "You want to find the right mix of diet and exercise that will make your body a machine for the days when you pitch."

Roger ran two miles every day between home and school. His weight came down to 200.

Roger won six straight games without a loss. But he was only the number 3 pitcher for Spring Woods. The team's star pitchers were Rick Luecken and Raymer Noble. Both threw around 90 miles an hour, at least 10 miles an hour faster than Roger's best.

But Roger could throw strikes "from morning to night," Coach Maiorana once said. Roger broke a school record by fanning seventeen of twenty-one batters in a seven-inning game. "Love those punchouts," he said of the seventeen strikeouts. Spring Woods won thirty-one of thirty-five games and finished among the state's top eight teams.

"You hardly ever walk a man," Coach Maiorana told Roger. "But you've got to throw harder to get the scouts interested."

Scouts signed Lueken and Noble to contracts. A Minnesota Twins scout talked to Roger. "We might sign you," the scout said. "But I can't promise you a lot of money. You don't throw hard enough."

In the fall of 1979 Roger lifted weights and "bulked up" to 220 pounds to play defensive end. A few colleges talked to him about playing football. But Roger told Randy, "If I am going to be a big-league athlete, I want to be a big-league pitcher."

In the spring of 1980 Coach Maiorana watched Roger run for hours in the outfield. Sweat streamed down his face. Roger wanted to drop back down to 200.

His friends watched him work out and shook their heads. "Crazy Roger," they told each other, "he never has any fun."

"I'm losing friends because I don't want to party with them," Roger told Randy. "I sacrifice a lot of good times for sports. But I've made a decision not to do alcohol or drugs with them."

On Friday nights he watched his friends roar off in cars to go to parties. Roger didn't own a car. Instead, on Friday nights he ran alone for hours in the hills near Katy, where he now lived with his mother and sisters. They had moved from Vandalia.

He wanted to build strength in his thighs and lower back. His legs, he told himself, could help him fling the ball at 90 miles an hour. He had forgotten that something else has to fling the ball—the arm.

Luecken and Noble were gone. Roger, now a senior, became Spring Woods' no. 1 pitcher. In one game, he struck out eighteen batters. "He's not fast," the Twins scout said one day to a craggy-faced man sitting next to him. "But he sure gets the ball over the plate."

"To me," said the craggy-faced man, "getting the ball over

On the mound for the Gators, Roger always kept his eyes fixed on the strike zone as he threw.

the plate comes first, then 90-mile-an-hour velocity. If you throw strikes, a batter has to swing or it's a called strike. If he misses, it's a strike. If he hits the ball, nine men are trying to get him out."

The craggy-faced man had once hit in the big leagues for the Philadelphia Phillies and New York Mets. His name was Wayne Graham. He had just taken over as the baseball coach at Houston's San Jacinto Junior College.

Roger won thirteen and lost five. Spring Woods came within a game of winning its district championship. Roger also pitched on weekends for an American Legion team that almost won the state championship.

The Twins scout came to Roger's home. "You don't throw hard enough for any other big-league team to be interested in you," he said. "We'll take a chance and give you a thousand dollars."

Roger knew he could not do much for his mother with a thousand dollars. But his face turned pale when the scout said, "You will never get another chance to pitch in the big leagues."

That was the night Roger jogged through the streets of Katy. That was the night he stretched out on a pitcher's mound and stared upward at the stars. That was the night he wondered if his dream of pitching in the big leagues had vanished. That was the night he told himself, "I'll show 'em; I'll show 'em."

A few weeks later Wayne Graham called.

Chapter 2

Roger stood on the mound. Coach Graham crouched behind the catcher at home plate on a fall day in 1980. A few weeks earlier Roger had accepted Coach Graham's offer to come to San Jacinto Junior College, where students graduated in two years.

No four-year big-name college had offered Roger a baseball scholarship, which gave an athlete a college education at no cost. So Roger had gladly accepted Coach Graham's offer of a free education at San Jacinto. He hoped that scouts from big-name colleges might see him pitch and offer him a scholarship next year. And the San Jacinto campus stood only a short car ride from his mother's home in Katy, so he didn't have to leave his family. He could study business at San Jacinto. If he didn't get the chance to play in the big leagues, he could get a job in business to support his mother.

Coach Graham held a radar gun in his hand. He pointed the gun at the mound. The gun measured the speed of Roger's pitches. "Let me see your best fast ball, Roger," the coach shouted. "Really air it out."

Roger wound up and threw. The ball slammed into the catcher's mitt. "Eighty-two miles an hour," Graham shouted. "And you're not even using all of your arm."

Roger stared at the coach. What did he mean?

That afternoon the coach showed Roger video tapes of his pitching motion. "See there," the coach said. "You try to do everything with your body. Your arm sort of just comes along for the ride. You've got to keep the arm moving toward the hitter even after you let go of the ball. You've got to finish strong."

During the next month Roger threw every day. From

The eighteen-year-old pitcher for the San Jacinto Gators still looks like the schoolboy pitcher for Spring Woods High.

behind the batting cage he heard Graham's loud roar, "Finish strong! Finish strong!"

That winter the eighteen-year-old Roger grew taller and stronger. "I am coming together physically," he told Randy. He had grown now to six-foot-four and weighed 215 pounds.

"In high school," Randy told him, "you were 220 pounds, but lots of it was baby fat. Now there's muscle. All that running you did, all those exercises, now they're paying off."

Baseball practice started in the late winter of 1981. One day Roger threw a pitch and heard an assistant coach shout, "You broke 90, Roger, you broke 90."

Roger couldn't believe he had thrown a fast ball faster than 90 miles an hour. He made the coach show him the speed on the radar gun's screen.

"You've got genius control and now you've got super velocity," Graham told Roger. "Not many have both—only a few like Tom Seaver and Sandy Koufax. The great ones."

Roger liked to watch one of the great ones—Nolan Ryan. The Houston Astros had obtained Nolan Ryan from the California Angels. No one, said some sportswriters, had ever thrown a baseball as fast as Ryan. "The Ryan Express," as they called his fast ball, had been measured at 100-plus miles an hour.

Roger and Randy often went to the Houston Astrodome two hours before a game to watch Ryan warm up on days when he wasn't pitching. Roger sat in a grandstand seat, high above the field, and stared wide-eyed as the Ryan Express roared into a catcher's mitt. Roger loved to hear the crack of the ball hitting the mitt. He imagined himself throwing 100-mile-an-hour fast balls at big-league hitters like Reggie Jackson.

Nolan Ryan. Tom Seaver. Sandy Koufax. Reggie Jackson. The great ones. For the first time Roger began to imagine that he could be more than a big-league pitcher. "Maybe," he told himself, "I can be one of the great ones."

When the 1981 baseball season began, San Jacinto immediately became a team other junior colleges hated to play. San Jacinto's number 1 pitcher, Roger Clemens, was feared as the pitcher who could knock the bat out of a hitter's hands—"that's how hard he throws," other players said.

One afternoon the San Jacinto Gators rode in their school bus across flat desert land for a game against Bee County. Roger knew he would pitch that night. He stared out the window at the heat shimmering off the desert floor. He was glad the game would be played at night when the air would be cooler.

"Stop fooling around back there!" Coach Graham shouted at three of his players who were roughhousing in the back. Grinning sheepishly, the players immediately sat straight in their seats.

Minutes later, however, one of the players nudged another in the ribs. Again the three were roughhousing.

"Stop the bus!" Graham roared. He ordered the three out of the bus. He pointed to distant light towers. "There's the ballpark," Graham said. "You'll walk to the game."

Roger opened the bus door. He stepped out so the three offenders could file past him. But before Roger could leap back into the bus, the driver stepped on the gas pedal. The bus roared down the road.

Hot, dusty air blew into the face of San Jacinto's starting pitcher. He and the other players trudged down the sun-baked road toward the faraway towers. Sweat splotched the backs of their baseball uniforms and glistened on their faces. They wearily came closer to the stadium. A sign read, "Rodeo Tonight." This was the wrong stadium.

An hour later the gasping Roger and his three teammates

climbed over the fence of the ballpark. Graham told Roger to get ready to pitch.

Roger struck out the first batter. He struck out the second. Watching on the bench, a teammate whistled softly and said, "And he's still tuckered out from that walk across the desert."

As the ninth inning began, no Bee County batter had stroked a hit off Roger. He stood within three outs of pitching his first no-hitter.

Roger struck out the first batter. The second lofted a high popup that a San Jacinto infielder settled under and snared.

Taking a deep breath, Roger whizzed a 95-mile-an-hour fast ball at the last batter between him and his first no-hitter.

Roger (center) is congratulated by teammates after a Gator victory.

The batter lurched away from the inside pitch and swung feebly at the ball. The ball hit the handle of his bat and fluttered over the infield. It dropped inches away from an infielder's glove for a single.

Roger won the game, giving up only that one hit. One day, he told himself, he'd pitch a no-hitter.

He won nine games and lost only two that 1981 season. San Jacinto came within one game of going to the Junior College World Series. Sportswriters picked Roger to the 1981 Junior College All-American team.

His phone rang constantly. College coaches called from Florida to California. No big-college coach had wanted him a year ago. But now that he could throw faster than 90 miles an hour, everyone wanted him.

Big-league scouts looked at him with shining eyes. A New York Mets scout called Roger and told him, "The Mets will be in Houston next week. Our manager Joe Torre and pitching coach Bob Gibson want to watch you throw. Meet them at the Astrodome."

Roger walked onto the Astrodome field, wearing a Met uniform. He looked up into the grandstand seats where he had sat listening to Nolan Ryan's fast ball. Now he stood on the same field with Nolan Ryan.

Roger walked to the visiting team's bullpen. For fifteen minutes he threw fast balls that smacked into a catcher's glove.

The Mets thought they had seen faster pitchers. But they decided to offer Roger $25,000 to sign a contract. They would send him, an official told Roger, to a minor-league team. "You could be in the big leagues in two or three years," the official said.

Roger said no. His mother wanted him to go to college. "If

baseball doesn't work out for you," she said, "you will have a good education."

"You were right when you said no to that Twins scout who offered only a thousand dollars," Roger said. "And I think you're still giving me good advice."

Roger knew that big-league teams were offering $100,000 and more to pitchers who could throw 90 miles an hour. Higher offers than $25,000 would come, Roger told Randy and his mother. Anyway, he said, he wanted to be a Longhorn.

University of Texas coach Cliff Gustafson had offered Roger a scholarship. The Texas Longhorns baseball team nearly always stood in the nation's Top Ten teams. Lots of

University of Texas coach Cliff Gustafson shakes Roger's hand after a victory.

Texas boys yearned to wear the uniform of the Texas Longhorns—and Roger was one of them.

Roger walked slowly off the field. He was the losing pitcher. The University of Miami had edged the Longhorns and Roger, 2–1, in the final game of the 1982 College World Series.

"Those two runs were unearned," his two best buddies on the team, shortstop Spike Owen and pitcher Calvin Schiraldi, told him.

"I know those two runs came in on errors," Roger said, "but they still beat us."

The University of Texas team flew back to its campus in Austin. Roger knew that Spike, the team's best hitter, would graduate in a few weeks. Soon, in fact, Spike would sign a major-league contract with the Seattle Mariners.

"We'll miss Spike's bat and glove next year," Roger told Calvin. "But you and I can pitch Texas to the top in 1983."

Teammates called Roger "the Goose." They said he whooshed fast balls as fast as big-league fireballer Goose Gossage. They called Calvin "the Nibbler" because he threw curves that nibbled the corners of the plate for strikes.

In 1983 the Nibbler won fourteen games and the Goose won thirteen. Roger struck out 151 batters in 166 innings—and walked only 22. "He throws more strikes than any college pitcher I ever saw," his coach said.

The Longhorns flew to Omaha, Nebraska, for the 1983 College World Series. More than fifty big-league scouts watched the games from behind home plate.

Calvin beat James Madison College, 12–1. Roger beat Oklahoma State, 9–1. Calvin won again. On a cool June night Roger strode to the mound of a packed stadium. He faced the

University of Alabama and its star slugger, third baseman Dave Magadan, for the championship.

"Clemens doesn't have the heart to win close games," one scout said to another. "He's fast for six or seven innings. Then he slows down. I think he loses heart when he has to win a close one."

Texas jumped out to a 2–0 lead. In the fourth Alabama put runners on second and third. The brawny Magadan came to the plate. Roger threw a fast ball on the outside. A left-handed hitter, Magadan lunged for the pitch. He slapped a drive down the left field line for a double. That hit tied the game, 2–2.

"See," said the scout, "Clemens gives up runs in close games. No heart."

"I think his arm is tired from too much pitching in junior college and college ball," said another scout.

Alabama scored another run. But Texas came back with two. Roger strode to the mound for the top of the eighth. He had to protect a thin 4–3 lead.

Roger struck out the first hitter. The second popped up the ball to a Texas infielder. Roger struck out the third. And in the ninth, with the crowd roaring at each pitch, Roger struck out the first batter, the second—and the third.

Texas had won the series. Calvin Schiraldi hugged Roger. Dave Magadan shook Roger's hand.

All three had been watched closely by the major-league scouts. Some still thought that Roger had no heart, even after seeing him strike out the last three batters to win a close one-run battle against Alabama for the championship.

A few weeks before the series, a Boston Red Sox scout, the square-jawed Joe Morgan, flew to the Texas campus in Austin to see if the reports were true. He watched Calvin Schiraldi win a game. After the last out, Morgan walked toward the exit. He saw a Longhorn catcher come onto the

Roger leaps high into the air after striking out the last Alabama batter in the 1983 College World Series.

field from the dugout. Morgan stopped. He saw Roger follow the catcher, wearing a glove and holding a ball. Roger was going to work out.

Morgan sat down. He watched Roger thump fast balls into the catcher's mitt. "He's throwing 90-mile-an-hour fast balls," Morgan told himself. "That's no tired arm."

Roger often pitched on Friday nights, Morgan discovered. Then he came in to relieve late in games on Saturday. His arm weary, he gave up runs as a reliever in those close games in which he loved to pitch.

"That kid has a great heart," Morgan told Sox officials.

The Red Sox officials decided to make Roger their first

Roger and his Longhorn buddy Calvin Schiraldi would be teammates again when both were signed to the Boston Red Sox.

pick in the 1983 draft. The Mets chose Calvin Schiraldi and Dave Magadan.

Roger finally signed a big-league contract—for $120,000. He gave much of the money to his mother. His childhood dream—that he could support her—had come true.

The Red Sox sent Roger to their Class A league Winter Haven, Florida, team. Roger had hoped to pitch for a Class AA team. The highest minor league is Class AAA, the stepping stone to the majors. Roger set a goal: to pitch for a Class AA team within a year.

He rose at seven each morning to run for miles while his teammates snoozed. Each afternoon he opened the gates of the ballpark while his teammates watched TV in their hotel rooms. He twisted and turned for an hour of exercising and weight lifting, strengthening legs and arms, while his teammates strolled leisurely to the ballpark.

"Lots of guys," he said, "are happy to play in the minors. I want to get to the majors as fast as I can."

Roger had played before crowds of 20,000 in college. Here at Winter Haven he played before rows of empty seats. He could hear a cough in the bleachers. When a fan shouted, "You're a bum!" a player could turn and pick out the fan who had insulted him.

"One nice thing about playing in an empty park," Roger often told friends. "You know who is for you and who is against you."

Roger won two and lost one in his first three starts. In his fourth start he shut out the Lakeland Tigers, striking out fifteen. The next morning he heard a knocking at his hotel-room door. Roger looked through a peephole. He saw the face of Ed Kenny, the top Red Sox scout.

"I hope I didn't do anything wrong," Roger said to himself. He opened the door.

Chapter 3

"Pack your bags, Roger," said Ed Kenny, holding a cigar. "You're on your way to double-A."

Three days later Roger stood on New England soil for the first time in his life. He wore the uniform of the New Britain (Connecticut) Red Sox. Roger won two games in a row as the Red Sox made the Eastern League playoffs.

To get to the finals, New Britain had to beat the Reading Phils. Roger won of three New Britain victories, striking out fifteen Phils. After the game the Reading manager told reporters, "That Clemens is too good for this league."

New Britain took on the Lynn Pirates for the league championship. New Britain won two games. Roger pitched the third. He struck out ten, blanking the Pirates, 6–0. For the second time in only three months, Roger stood in the clubhouse of a championship team.

In half a season of pro ball, Roger had won nine and lost two. In 98 innings he had walked only fourteen and struck out 108. He finished with a low 1.19 earned-run average. Earned-run average, or ERA, is the number of runs scored against a pitcher each nine innings, not counting runs that come in on errors.

"You've got one of the best records of any minor-league pitcher," a Boston Red Sox official told Roger. The Sox were limping toward a dismal sixth-place finish.

"You can join the team at Fenway Park," the Sox official told Roger. "You won't get to pitch, but you can work out with the team for the last two weeks of the season."

Roger walked into the carpeted, high-ceilinged Red Sox clubhouse. Awe in his eyes, he looked at the closetlike dressing stalls where Hall of Famers like Ted Williams and Carl Yastrzemski once dressed.

A clubhouse man handed Roger his shiny white Red Sox uniform. Its number was 21. That was Roger's favorite number. Randy had worn 21 in college. Roger wore 21 as a Longhorn. And 21 would soon become the favorite number of a girl back in Houston.

Roger had known Debbie Godfrey when both were students at Spring Woods High. But they had never dated. Roger and Debbie met again when he came back to Katy from Boston after the 1983 season. On October 21, 1983, they went out on a date for the first time.

"I want to become a Dallas Cowboy cheerleader next fall," the slim, dark-haired girl told Roger.

"I hope to be pitching for the Red Sox next spring."

"I'll be in football," Debbie said, "and you'll be in baseball. But we'll both be in the big leagues."

Debbie could fly over gymnastic bars. She churned across swimming pools. She and Roger began to run together in the mornings. Debbie was practicing to pass physical tests to be a Cowboy cheerleader.

By Christmas time Roger was dating only Debbie. When he left for spring training in February 1984, he promised to write. But he didn't. He phoned her from Winter Haven every day, and they talked for hours.

At Winter Haven Roger worked hard to throw a slider. A slider starts out like a fast ball, then breaks left or right. "The slider can get me more strikeouts because batters will be fooled," Roger told Debbie. "They'll think it's a fast ball."

But sometimes his slider hung in the air instead of breaking. Hitters slam hanging sliders for home runs.

Batters began to rap Roger's hanging sliders in spring training games. The Red Sox manager, Ralph Houk, decided to send Roger to a Class AAA club. "You'll go to Pawtucket where you can improve that slider," Houk told Roger.

Roger's chin fell. He had been sure he would go north to

Debbie Clemens watches from the stands as Roger pitches at Fenway Park.

Boston and "the bigs," as players call the majors. He phoned Debbie. "Don't worry," she said. "You'll be pitching for the Red Sox before the 1984 season ends."

Pitching for the Pawtucket (Rhode Island) Red Sox, Roger threw lots of sliders and curves. Mixing fast balls, sliders, and curves, Roger struck out ten batters in one game.

The next day Debbie called him. She had slipped and broken an elbow. Her dream of becoming a Cowboy cheerleader had vanished.

Roger flew home to comfort her. He told Debbie she would soon have full use of the arm. After cheering up Debbie, Roger asked her to be his wife. She said yes. They would get married at the end of the season.

Back in Pawtucket, Roger threw sliders that broke away inside and curves that broke downward. His fast balls burst by batters like bolts of lightning. He struck out fifty batters in forty-six innings.

Early in May the phone rang in Roger's hotel room in Pawtucket. "Fly to Kansas City tonight," a Red Sox vice president told him. "You're joining the big team."

Four days later, on May 15, 1984, Roger nervously stood on the mound in Cleveland's huge Municipal Stadium. In the stands sat Debbie, Randy, and Roger's mother. They had flown to Cleveland to see Roger pitch his first big-league game.

The Indians knew the rookie righthander was nervous. They watched his fast balls sail wide of the plate. Roger walked three batters, a high number for him. When he threw pitches down the middle, Indians slammed line drives to all fields. They led, 5–0, after four innings.

The Sox rallied, closing the gap to 5–4 in the fifth. Then Roger got into more trouble. Liners sang by his ears.

The broad-chested Ralph Houk walked slowly to the

mound. He took the ball from Roger. Debbie, Randy, and his mom stood and applauded as Roger walked quickly to the dugout. In the next day's paper Roger read that his fast ball had been clocked at 96 miles an hour.

A week later Roger lasted seven innings, leaving ahead, 5–3. Reliever Bob Stanley came on to save Roger's first big-league victory.

"You've got great control and velocity," pitching coach Lee Stange told Roger. "But when you throw pitches down the middle, big-league hitters will hit even 95-mile-an-hour fast balls. Use that control to nick the corners of the plate."

By mid-August Roger had won seven and lost four. The

Roger strides forward, pushing off his back leg, as he pitches against the Minnesota Twins to win his first big-league game.

Red Sox pitching staff—Roger, Bobby Ojeda, Bruce Hurst, Dennis "Oil Can" Boyd, and Al Nipper—was being called the best young staff in the league.

On August 21—that lucky number again—Roger had his best day ever. He beat the Royals, 11–1, striking out fifteen without walking a batter. He became only the fourth pitcher in big-league history to strike out fifteen and walk nobody.

His record now 9–4, Roger faced the Indians on August 31. By the fourth inning he had struck out seven batters. Maybe, he told himself, he could strike out sixteen.

Slugger Andre Thornton stood at the plate. Roger decided, as he liked to say, "to really air out my fastball." He threw as hard as he could—and pain shot up his right arm.

Roger grabbed the arm. Ralph Houk dashed out of the dugout. "What's wrong?" the manager asked, frowning.

"I think I hurt my arm!" the young pitcher replied.

"Nothing more than a strained tendon in the arm," a doctor told Roger the next day. But Houk told Roger to rest the arm. Roger didn't pitch again in 1984. He finished the season with a 9–4 record.

At spring training in March 1985, Roger told reporters that his arm felt fine. The Red Sox had finished fourth in 1984. Reporters predicted that the team could finish first in the American League East in 1985 with its corps of young pitchers. A bunch of hard hitters filled the lineup, including third baseman Wade Boggs and outfielders Jim Rice and Dwight Evans.

Roger came to the Red Sox spring training camp at Winter Haven with Mrs. Roger Clemens. He and Debbie had been married. One of the ushers at the ceremony was Calvin Schiraldi, now a Met minor leaguer. Roger and Debbie flew to Hawaii for their honeymoon. Their seat numbers on the plane—that old lucky number again—were 21A and 21B.

That spring Roger lifted weights to strengthen his arms and shoulders as well as his upper thighs. Like a future Hall of Famer, Tom Seaver, Roger believed that by thrusting toward home plate with his legs, a pitcher added velocity to his fast ball.

The Sox had a new manager, the rangy John McNamara, and a new pitching coach, Bill Fischer. The burly Fischer watched Roger throw fast balls.

"You hold the ball so your fingers line up with the seams," Fischer said. "That makes your fast ball sink. Try holding the ball across the seams. That will make your fast ball jump."

Soon Roger knew how to make his fast ball rise by

Roger throws a strike as he fans one of fifteen Kansas City Royals later in his 1984 rookie season.

holding the ball so his fingers lined up with the seams. Or he could make it dive. Batters had to guess where the ball would go—up or down—as it exploded toward them at 95 miles an hour.

"Take it easy," McNamara warned Roger as the 1985 season began. "Don't try to throw the ball through walls and strain your arm again."

But opposing batters slugged Roger's slowed-up fast balls. He lost three out of four. But then he shut out Cleveland, striking out ten. That night he told Debbie, "Now I'm close to putting it all together."

But his arm began to feel heavy. Pain stung his right shoulder. The Red Sox told him to rest. Throwing in a bullpen, Roger whizzed 95-mile-an-hour fast balls. But he could throw that fast for only a few minutes. Then the arm ached.

Roger wanted to pitch. "The pain has got to go away if I throw hard enough," he told Debbie. But she knew he worried that his career might be ended before it had really begun.

He won a game. His arm, he told Randy, "still doesn't feel right." He had won seven and lost five. His ERA was a respectable 3.29.

One day he warmed up to pitch against California. He told himself the arm would stop aching. Bill Fischer saw Roger wince as he threw. The coach told Roger someone else would start.

Roger strode angrily into the clubhouse. He ripped off his uniform. Al Nipper ran after him. "You're not finished," Al told Roger. Al saw tears of rage in Roger's eyes.

That summer Roger rested the arm. He tried to pitch against the Yankees. From the dugout John McNamara could see that Roger was in pain.

McNamara ran to the mound. "I'm not worried about

36

winning this stupid game," the manager told Roger. The Sox were headed toward a fifth-place finish in the AL East. "I'm worried about you and your career."

Roger trudged to the dugout. The next day he and Debbie flew to Columbus, Georgia, where a doctor examined the arm. "We will have to operate to see what the trouble is," the doctor said.

"For the past two seasons," Debbie said, "it seems it's just been setback, setback, setback."

Chapter 4

"Can you throw a fast ball without any pain?" catcher Rick Gedman asked Roger.

They were standing on the field at Winter Haven early in March 1986. The Columbus surgeon had taken a torn bit of mushy cartilage out of Roger's right shoulder. Roger was lifting weights to strengthen the shoulder.

"There's no pain," Roger told Gedman. "But my fast ball isn't what it was."

In spring training games Roger threw sliders and slow curves. "I'm a junk ball pitcher now," he said, bitterness in his voice. Batters slugged those junk pitches for long home runs.

"Throw a fast ball," Bill Fischer shouted to Roger one day. Fischer stood behind the plate holding a radar gun.

Roger threw. "How fast?" Fischer asked.

"Around 80," Roger said glumly.

"You're throwing 93!" Fischer shot back.

Roger's face brightened. He began to run even harder and lift weights longer.

"He always worked hard," Gedman told someone. "But he

was like a demon after what Fischer told him. I think he thought, 'Here's my second chance and I'm not going to let it slip away.' "

"Up to now," Debbie said that spring, "Roger feels he hasn't been able to show what he can do. He wants to accomplish so much. He wants to be the best ever. He's never satisfied. If he pitches a one-run game and strikes out ten, he wants next to pitch a shutout and strike out fifteen."

Sportswriters picked the 1986 Red Sox to finish fourth or fifth in the AL East. And many thought that Roger was just another pitcher who always had a sore arm.

Roger won his first three games, beating Chicago, Kansas City, and Detroit. He struck out ten Tigers. "A lot of hard work," he said, "has paid off."

On April 29 he went to the mound at Fenway Park to seek his fourth straight victory of 1986. Almost three hours later he had walked into baseball's all-time record book.

Spike Owen gripped the bat as he stood at the plate. He eyed Roger, his old Longhorn buddy, who stood high on the mound. Spike, now the Seattle Mariners' shortstop, was leading off in the first inning of this April 29 game at Fenway.

Roger threw a fast ball that dived. He threw a fast ball that jumped. He threw a slider that broke away. Spike fanned. Roger struck out the next two hitters. The Red Sox fans roared after each whiff.

Roger struck out two Mariners in the second and one in the third. After each strikeout, Debbie—seated behind home plate—threw her arms into the air. Her arms would be kept busy this night.

A teenage fan began to tape sheets of paper onto the wall of the centerfield bleachers. He marked each sheet with a big K. The letter K is scoring shorthand for a strikeout.

The teenager had strung twelve Ks in a row by the end of

the fifth inning. Neither team had scored. By the seventh the row of Ks had grown to sixteen—but the Mariners led, 1–0. The Mariners' Gorman Thomas had slammed a home run.

Roger knew he had to keep on striking out Mariners if he hoped to win. He also knew that the major-league record for strikeouts in a nine-inning game was nineteen. The record was held by Steve Carlton, Tom Seaver, and Roger's boyhood hero, Nolan Ryan.

In the bottom of the seventh, two Red Sox runners stood on base. Dwight Evans waited for the pitch. The rangy Evans boomed a long drive. Seated in the dugout, Roger peeked

Roger twists off a pitch against Seattle at Fenway Park on the night of April 29, 1986.

between the arms of teammates. He watched the drive soar toward the fence, hoping . . . hoping . . .

Home run! The Sox led, 3–1.

Roger went to the mound for the eighth. He struck out two more for a total of eighteen.

As Roger stepped into the dugout, Al Nipper said, "You're two strikeouts from twenty and the record."

"Don't put pressure on Roger," a Sox player growled.

Al Nipper smiled. "Roger loves pressure," he said.

Spike Owen led off in the ninth. As Roger wound up, Red Sox players chanted from the dugout, "One...two...three ...BLASTOFF!"

Boston fans hold up signs marked with K's to show their pride in Roger.

Roger holds the last baseball he threw in the twenty-strikeout game against Seattle.

Blastoff is the word heard at Cape Canaveral when a rocket blasts off into space. Roger, said the players, was blasting off rockets at the Mariner hitters tonight.

Owen struck out. No. 19. That tied the big-league record.

Outfielder Phil Bradley came up to hit. Roger wound up to throw. He heard the chant, "One . . . two . . . BLASTOFF!"

Bradley swung and missed. Strike one! He swung and missed. Strike two . . .

"One . . . two . . . three . . . BLASTOFF!" The 95-mile-an-hour fast ball whizzed by Bradley.

Strike three! Roger had twenty strikeouts—and a record even bigger than he had imagined.

Roger had not walked a single batter. No one in more than 100 years of big-league baseball history had ever fanned twenty batters and walked no one.

The next day, when Roger walked into the Sox clubhouse, he saw a sign posted over his locker: ROCKET MAN. He had a nickname that would stick.

The Rocket Man later told Debbie, "Now I've really got a chance to be where I want someday to be—the Hall of Fame."

Chapter 5

"The Streak."

Every fan in America was talking about Roger's streak as spring turned into the summer of 1986. After that twenty-strikeout victory over the Mariners, Roger reeled off ten more straight victories. His record stood at fourteen victories, no defeats.

The American League record for consecutive victories at the start of the season was fifteen. On July 2, at Fenway Park, Roger strode to the mount to pitch against the Toronto Blue Jays and go for that record.

Roger led, 2–1, as the eighth inning began. Roger walked a batter. Another stroked a single. With one out, runners stood on first and second.

"One . . . two . . . three . . . BLASTOFF!" shouted Sox players at their Rocket Man.

A lefty hitter, Rance Mulliniks, stood at the plate. Roger threw a 95-mile-an-hour fast ball. Mulliniks stuck out his bat and popped the ball into left field. The ball rolled to the corner for a double that tied the game, 2–2.

Manager John McNamara hurried to the mound. Roger looked tired, he thought. McNamara waved in reliever Bob Stanley. The Blue Jays scored two more runs to win, 4–2. For the first time in 1986, Roger saw the letters LP, meaning "losing pitcher," next to his name in the next day's box score.

Roger won three of his next five. In one game he struck out a batter to end the inning. Al Nipper met Roger at the dugout. "The radar gun measured that last pitch at 100 miles an hour," Al told Roger.

Roger sat down. He could hardly believe what he had just heard. He had thrown a ball as fast as Nolan Ryan.

Two of Roger's University of Texas buddies, Calvin Schiraldi and Spike Owen now wore Red Sox uniforms. Calvin came from the Mets and won games as a reliever. Spike came from the Mariners and slugged line drives. The Red Sox held onto first place, but the Tigers and Yankees nipped at their heels.

Roger set off on another streak. He won seven games in a row. The Sox pulled away to win the American League Eastern title.

Roger finished the season with twenty-four wins and only four losses. He gave up only 2.48 earned runs a game, the league's best.

The California Angels won the American League West. In the first game of the playoffs, the Angels beat Roger, 8–1. "Let's face it," Debbie said later. "Roger has pitched a lot of innings this season. His arm is tired."

The Angels went ahead, two games to one. Roger tried to pitch with only three days' rest. His fastball numbed the bats of the Angel hitters for eight innings and he led, 3–0, as the ninth inning began.

Roger couldn't put muscle on his fast ball any longer. His fast balls came in as straight as a string. The Angels' Doug

DeCinces boomed a homer. Roger got one out and stood only two outs away from his first postseason victory.

The next two batters slapped singles. McNamara took Roger out. The Angels tied the game in the ninth, 3–3, and won in the eleventh.

The Angels now led, three games to one. They led in the fifth game, 5–2, in the ninth inning. They stood only two outs away from winning the pennant.

But the Angels never won that pennant. The Sox roared back with four runs in the ninth and won, 7–6, to stay alive.

The Sox won the sixth game. Roger went to the mount at Fenway for the seventh do-or-die game.

Roger shut out the Angels for seven innings. The Sox led, 8–0. But all those innings of pitching in this series had worn him down. His knees quivered. "His face," catcher Rick Gedman said later, "looked as white as a mummy's."

The Angels led off the eighth with a hit. Calvin Schiraldi came in from the bullpen to relieve Roger just as Roger had relieved him back in Texas. Calvin struck out five Angels in two innings, and Boston won the game, 8–1, and the American League pennant.

Roger shivered under a blanket in the Sox clubhouse as players whooped around him. A doctor told him he was exhausted. But in a few days, Roger knew, he had to go up against the champions of the National League—the heavy-hitting New York Mets—in his first World Series.

The Series opened at Shea Stadium in New York. The Red Sox won the first game, 1–0. Calvin Schiraldi came out of the bullpen to save the game for starter Bruce Hurst.

Roger started the second game. The Mets' starter was their strikeout ace, Dwight Gooden. The Red Sox teed off on Gooden's fast balls, scoring six runs in five innings. The Mets scored twice off Roger in the third inning. As the Mets came to bat in the fifth, the Red Sox led, 6–2. In the fifth Roger gave up a walk and a single. McNamara came to the mound and told Roger he looked tired. "To tell you the truth," Debbie said later, "Roger was tired late in the season." The Red Sox won, 9–3, but Roger had not pitched enough innings to earn the victory.

Ahead two games to none, the Red Sox came into Fenway Park for the third game dreaming of the team's first world championship since 1918. But the Mets won the next two games to tie the series at two games apiece. In the fifth game, the Red Sox again beat Dwight Gooden, 4–2, and the Sox went back to New York ahead, three games to two.

Roger started the sixth game against Bobby Ojeda. As the Mets came to bat in the bottom of the seventh inning, the Red Sox led, 3–2. Roger got one out, then a second out.

Met center fielder Mookie Wilson came to bat. Roger threw a slider. Wilson lunged at the pitch and hit a lazy fly to center field. Roger turned to watch the center fielder catch the ball.

Then he looked at the middle finger of his pitching hand. He saw blood. Roger had ripped his fingernail when he threw the slider. In the dugout John McNamara saw the blood. "Does it sting?" he asked.

"Sure, it stings," Roger said. But he told McNamara he could pitch at least one more inning throwing a lot of fast balls. He knew the Red Sox needed only six more outs to win the world championship—and Roger wanted to be the winning pitcher of that championship game.

McNamara stared at the bloody finger. He wondered if Roger could get those last six outs. In the top of the eighth the Red Sox's Dave Henderson led off with a base hit. A bunt moved him to second. It was Roger's turn to hit. McNamara decided to put in a pinch hitter for Roger.

Roger wished he could have stayed in the game, especially when the pinch hitter failed to score the runner. But the Sox still led, 3–2, as Calvin Schiraldi came to the mound in the bottom of the eighth inning to replace Roger. The Mets scored a run to tie the game, 3–3.

The game went into extra innings. In the top of the tenth the Red Sox scored twice to lead, 5–3.

Schiraldi retired the first two Mets in the bottom of the tenth. But in one of the most amazing comebacks in World Series history, the Mets scored three runs off Schiraldi for a dramatic 6–5 victory.

Roger swings at a pitch in batting practice before the second game of the 1986 World Series against the Mets.

Roger hurls a fast ball in the sixth game of the 1986 World Series against the New York Mets.

Roger went to the bullpen for the seventh game. He hoped he could come in as a relief pitcher if the Sox needed him. He watched glumly as the Mets took the lead, 6–3. In the eighth inning he jumped up, cheering, when Red Sox outfielder Dwight Evans socked a homer with a man on base. Now the Red Sox trailed by only a run, 6–5.

Roger hoped he could pitch the ninth. But McNamara chose Al Nipper. Met slugger Darryl Strawberry stroked a fast ball into the right-field seats. The Mets won the game, 8–5, and became the 1986 World Series champions.

Roger trudged to the clubhouse. The Red Sox had come so close to winning the world championship. But they were American League champs. And Roger would soon win three prizes he would treasure the rest of his life.

"It's a boy!"

Roger shouted the news to Randy and his mother. They stood in the corridor of a Houston hospital. Debbie had just given birth to their first child. The boy's name would be Koby. His first initial, K, would be a way for Koby Clemens to remember his dad's record-setting twenty Ks.

A few days earlier, the nation's baseball writers had named Roger the American League's best pitcher, giving him the 1986 Cy Young Award. "Why not?" said Boston fans. "He was our most valuable player."

That kind of talk set off angry arguments among fans, players, and reporters. Should a pitcher like Roger also be awarded the league's Most Valuable Player Award? Many players said no. "A pitcher gets into only thirty or thirty-five games a year," they said. "He can't be as valuable as a hitter who plays in more than a hundred games during a season." But others argued, "Would the Red Sox have won the pennant without Roger? You know the answer is no. He has got to be the most valuable player."

The nation's sportswriters agreed with that view. A few weeks later they named Roger the American League's Most Valuable Player. He was the first pitcher in fifteen years to win the MVP award.

Off-season, Roger liked to fly to sunny resorts like Key West. He loved to water ski, swim, fish, or lie on a beach. He stared at the wonders of Disney World. And he took baby Koby to toy stores and bought whatever toy Koby pointed a finger at.

Roger lifts the Most Valuable Player trophy awarded to him after the 1986 American League versus National League All-Star game in 1986.

He liked to talk about music, especially drums, which he liked to play. Often he slipped into the garage next to his home in Katy. He tinkered with the engines of his sports car and his Jeep. In the afternoons he often relaxed by watching his favorite TV show, *All My Children.*

"You won't hear Roger talking much about politics or what some congressman said on TV," a friend once remarked. "But he does like to talk to Little Leaguers about how to play baseball." During the off season Roger often talked about baseball to Coach Maiorana's Spring Woods players. Each January he went back to the University of Texas to pitch in the annual varsity-alumni baseball game.

Roger and Debbie attended church each Sunday. Often Roger spoke at his church's father-son dinners. Once a friend asked Roger, "If you could go back in history, what major event would you like to witness?"

"The birth of Christ," Roger said.

When the 1987 season began, Boston fans talked excitedly about winning a second straight pennant. But by June the fans were talking about Roger, asking, "What's wrong with Clemens?" So far he had won only four games while losing six. In one game the Yankees drove off the mound with six runs in one inning.

Roger knew what the trouble was. He had skipped much of spring training. The Red Sox had offered him a $60,000 raise. But the Sox gave raises of $100,000 to other players. "I won the Most Valuable Player and Cy Young awards," Roger protested. "Why shouldn't I get what the others are getting?"

Roger finally signed for $400,000 a year. He worked extra hard to make up for lost spring training time. "If I get smooth in my delivery," he told Debbie, "I'll start throwing strikes again."

By July Roger was throwing fast balls that dived and

Eleven-month-old Koby and Debbie sit with Roger in their Katy home and admire his second straight Cy Young Award.

jumped. His curves and sliders broke nastily. He won five straight games. By mid-September his record had risen to sixteen wins and nine losses.

But the Red Sox lost more games than they won. They finished fifth. The Sox had traded away older, experienced players like Don Baylor, Dave Henderson, and Bill Buckner. "Younger players need older leaders," Roger said. "I know I do."

Near the end of that 1987 season Roger promised himself that he would win twenty games. He won his seventeenth, his eighteenth, then his nineteenth. On a cold, rainy afternoon at Fenway, he shut out the Brewers for his twentieth victory. Those twenty wins led the league. Two months later Roger won his second Cy Young Award. He became only the fourth pitcher to win the award twice in succession. One of the four, Jim Palmer, was on his way to the Hall of Fame. Another, Sandy Koufax, was already in the Hall of Fame.

As the 1988 season began, Roger could look back on a two-year record of forty-four victories and only thirteen defeats. He told friends, "I want to go to the Hall of Fame where the immortals are."

Chapter 6

The young Red Sox players were grumbling. Manager John McNamara, they told each other, favored the older players. "He yells at us," one young player said. "He never yells at the veterans."

Late in June 1988 the Red Sox were stumbling along ten games behind the Tigers and Yankees in the American League East. Red Sox hitters like Wade Boggs and Mike Greenwell slashed line drives, hitting .300 and higher. Roger had won nine and lost only three. His five shutouts led the league.

Early in July the Red Sox fired McNamara. The new manager was Joe Morgan, the former scout who had told the Sox to sign Roger and other young stars.

The happy young Red Sox slugged homers. Roger won six of his next eight games. The Red Sox suddenly seemed almost unbeatable. They won nineteen of their first twenty games under Morgan. They closed to within a game of the Tigers and Yankees.

Then, in August, Roger tried to lift a piece of furniture in his rented home near Boston. Pain streaked across his back.

Doctors told Roger he had to rest his shoulder. As Roger rested, the Tigers and Yankees pulled ahead of the Red Sox.

The rest cost Roger two or three starts and his chance to win a record third straight Cy Young Award. But early in September he pitched the first one-hitter of his big-league career to beat Cleveland, 6–0.

The Sox pulled ahead of the Yankees as the Tigers faded. But late in September the Yankees crept to within four and a half games of the Red Sox.

Boston fans nervously recalled the 1978 season. The Yankees came to Boston four games behind the Red Sox. The

The Rocket Man, his nickname marked on the collar of his turtleneck undershirt, shuts out the Yankees 6-0 late in the 1988 season.

Yankees swept a four-game series to force a tie. And in a playoff game for the Eastern Division title, the Yanks' Bucky Dent slammed a home run to win the game, 5–4, and the title.

To stop the Yankees late in this 1988 season, manager Joe Morgan sent Roger to the mound at Yankee Stadium. In the first inning the Yanks' Ricky Henderson slammed a liner straight at Roger. Roger tried to dodge, but the liner struck his right elbow. Joe Morgan ran to the mound. Could Roger continue to pitch?

The elbow felt numb, Roger said. But he insisted he could pitch. And he did, shutting out the Yanks, 6–0. A few days later the Red Sox clinched their second American League East championship in three years.

Roger had won eighteen and lost twelve. He led the league in strikeouts and shutouts. He tied Oakland's Dave Stewart for the most completed games—fourteen.

The Oakland As had won the American League West. In the playoffs for the pennant, the As beat Bruce Hurst in the first game. Roger started the second game. He held the As scoreless for six innings. The Red Sox led, 2–0.

In the seventh, an A's runner pranced off first base. The A's brawny slugger Jose Canseco waggled his bat, waiting for Roger's pitch. Roger looked at the runner. He figured the runner might steal. He knew he had to get the ball to the catcher quickly. Roger pitched too quickly to Canseco—and his foot slipped.

The pitch rode to the plate at only 80 miles an hour. Canseco drove the ball over the left-field wall for a homer that tied the score. The As picked away for another run to take the lead, 3–2.

Reliever Lee Smith replaced Roger as the eighth inning began. He gave up a run in the ninth and the As won, 5–4.

The As took the next two games to win the 1988

Roger shows his unhappiness after throwing a pitch that Oakland's Jose Canseco hit for a home run in the 1988 play off series against Oakland.

American League pennant. They went to the World Series to play the Dodgers—and lost.

"We're young. We'll be back to win other pennants," Roger told his teammates.

Roger went back to Katy with Debbie and their two children (another boy, Kory, had been born during the 1988 season). Just before the 1989 season began, a sportswriter asked catcher Rick Gedman if Roger really thought this team could win the pennant.

"Everybody wants to win," Gedman said. "But wanting to win burns much deeper in Roger than in other people. With Roger, it's always, 'I'll show you! I'll show you!' "

"When people say I can't do something," Roger once said, "I want to prove them wrong!" Roger began 1989 with a smile. He had just signed a three-year contract for $7.5 million. He had to smile even wider when he read that *Sports Illustrated* called the Red Sox "the best team in the field" in the American League East.

Why not? The Red Sox had four strong starting pitchers: Roger, Mike Boddicker, Wes Gardner, and John Dopson. And the Sox hitters like Wade Boggs, Nick Esasky, Ellis Burks, Mike Greenwell and Dwight Evans boomed the ball in spring-training games.

But Roger's smile faded during spring training. Wade Boggs was quoted in a magazine as saying that some Red Sox players did not like each other. Red Sox players glared at Boggs and at each other. Roger told sportswriters that he might hurt anyone who wrote bad things about what was most valuable to him—his family.

Roger won his first three decisions. He shut out Chicago, 11–0, whiffing eleven batters. That was the 34th time in his career that he had struck out ten or more in a game. But by June his fastball seemed to drag. Early in June he had won five, lost four. A sportswriter wrote: "There's something wrong with the Rocket Man."

There was. Roger had a torn a muscle near his right elbow. A swollen tendon in his right shoulder made him wince when he threw hard. But doctors said he needed only a week or so of rest and he would be back to normal.

By late August he seemed more than back to normal. He struck out thirteen Angels, his tops for 1989. That victory lifted the Sox to within four games of Toronto and Baltimore, who were tied for first.

Roger reminded himself not to throw so many fastballs.

Golfing near his Boston home, Roger watches one of his shots float toward the green.

"You can't pitch that way and last in this league," he said. "But my fastball is there when I want it."

The Sox began the September stretch run still only a few games behind Toronto and Baltimore. Over the past three seasons Roger had the best won-lost record (12–3) in September of any pitcher in baseball. Roger won three games, lost two in September of 1989. He finished with a 17–11 record. Mike Boddicker won fifteen, second-best on the staff. Dopson won twelve, Garner only three. The Red Sox led the league in hitting, but their pitching ranked only ninth in the fourteen-team league. The Red Sox finished third—six games behind Toronto.

Roger struck out 230 batters in 1989, second best in the league behind his boyhood idol, Nolan Ryan, still pitching strong at 42. Roger needed only 127 strikeouts—about half a season's total—to break the all-time Red Sox record for strikeouts. That record had been set in 1908.

Who set that 82-year-old record that Roger could break in the summer of 1990?

He was the pitcher whose name is engraved on the award that Roger yearned to win a record-breaking third time, Cy Young. Cy Young belonged to a select club that one day, very likely, the Rocket Man would join: the Hall of Fame.

CAREER STATISTICS

CAREER RECORD

YEAR	CLUB	G	IP	W	L	PCT	SO	BB	H	ERA
1983	Winter Haven	4	29	3	1	.750	36	0	22	1.24
1983	New Britain	7	52	4	1	.800	59	12	31	1.38
1983	Pawtucket	7	46 2/3	2	3	.400	50	14	39	1.93
1984	Boston	21	133 1/3	9	4	.692	126	29	146	4.32
1985	Boston	15	93 1/3	7	5	.583	74	37	83	3.29
1986	Boston	33	254	24	4	.857	238	67	179	2.48
1987	Boston	36	281 2/3	20	9	.690	256	83	248	2.97
1988	Boston	35	264	18	12	.600	291	62	217	2.93
1989	Boston	35	253 1/3	17	11	.607	230	93	215	3.13

Key to Table	
G	- Games Pitched
IP	- Inning Pitched per Season
W	- Wins
L	- Losses
PCT	- Percentage of Games Won
SO	- Strike Outs per Season
BB	- Base on Balls (Walks)
H	- Hits given up
ERA	- Earned Run Average per 9 Innings

Index

S

Seaver, Tom, 19
San Jacinto Junior College,
16, 19-22
Schiraldi, Calvin, 25, 28, 34,
45-48
Spring Woods High School,
13, 14, 30

U

University of Texas, 23-25, 45

W

Wilson, Mookie, 47